# 2006:2016
Selected Poems

Ashley Capes

*2006:2016*
Copyright Ashley Capes ©2017

Cover: Close-Up Books
Layout & Typset: Close-Up Books

All rights reserved. No part of this book may be reproduced in any form by any electronic or mechanical means including photocopying, recording, or information storage and retrieval without permission in writing from the authors.

ISBN-978-0-9876232-4-9

Published by Close-Up Books
Melbourne, Australia

*For Brooke*

# Acknowledgements

Poems in this collection were previously compiled in the following volumes:

*pollen and the storm* (2008)
Small Change Press & Ashley Capes
*stepping over seasons* (2009)
IP
*orion tips the saucepan* (2010)
Picaro Press
*between giants* (2012)
Ginninderra Press
*old stone: haiku, haibun & senryu* (2014)
Ginninderra Press
*7 Years* (2015)
Ginninderra Press
*VI* (2016)
Close-Up Books

Many of the works included in the books listed above (and also those which were previously uncollected) first appeared in the following publications, who I would like to thank for their support over the years:

*Island, Westerly, Going Down Swinging, fourW, Cordite Poetry Review, EMIT, Regional Poets Chapbook, idiom23, Moving Galleries, prospect 2, Speedpoets, miel magazine, Lot's Wife, Stylus Poetry Journal, Mascara Literary Review, Nibble Poetry, ARTrocity, foam:e, Poems & Pieces, Paper*

*Wasp, Peril, Haiku Dreaming, Notes from the Gean, World Haiku Review, Issa's Snail and The Renku Group, Colloquy, Black Rider Press, Verity La, Queen Vic Knives, Wet Ink, Modern Haibun and Tanka, 21D, Haibun Today, Third Australian Haiku Anthology, Paper Wasp, Shamrock, Heron's Nest, A Hundred Gourds, Contemporary Haibun Online, Haiku Bandit Society, Calico Cat Contest, Prune Juice, Acorn, Writ Poetry Review, Communion, Regime Magazine, Tincture, the grapple annual #2* and *Best Australian Poems 2012.*

Still other pieces were originally published online via my twitter account (@ash_capes) or my website (www.ashleycapes.com) and also at Medium.com.

# Contents

from *pollen and the storm*

| | |
|---|---|
| 11 | *pedestrian* |
| 12 | *hazel* |
| 13 | *31 Anderson Street* |
| 14 | *odd* |
| 15 | *sticks in milk* |
| 16 | *churchill* |
| 17 | *storm* |

from *stepping over seasons*

| | |
|---|---|
| 19 | *small town* |
| 20 | *on the road* |
| 22 | *echidna* |
| 23 | *august rain* |
| 24 | *all this ink* |
| 25 | *other objects* |
| 26 | *bianca* |
| 27 | *Bukowski and a wide range of landlords* |
| 28 | *bitches brew* |
| 29 | *eastern avenue* |
| 30 | *farm* |
| 31 | *botanic* |
| 33 | *by the curve* |
| 34 | *the jacket* |

from *orion tips the saucepan*

| | |
|---|---|
| 36 | *haiku & senryu* |

from *between giants*

- 41   *archaeological moment*
- 42   *transitions*
- 43   *birds still talking*
- 44   *now in the night*
- 46   *Keith Jarrett's scarecrow*
- 47   *man of cloth*
- 48   *yellows*
- 49   *a table set for thousands #2*
- 50   *man about town*
- 52   *stamped flat stamped*
- 53   *windstorm*
- 54   *concrete buttons*
- 55   *ridges in the skin*
- 56   *one of the townsfolk*
- 58   *stubble*

from *old stone: haiku, haibun & senryu*

- 60   *haiku & senryu*
- 63   *en route*
- 64   *temple*
- 65   *Firenze*
- 66   *Vatican Blues*
- 67   *night train*
- 68   *shade cloth*
- 69   *green skeletons*
- 70   *dovetails*

from *VI*

- 72   *even frogs could be happy*
- 73   *3885*

| | |
|---|---|
| 75 | *pink oceans* |
| 77 | *destined for mud* |
| 80 | *Beat Hero* |
| 81 | *super-8 sketches* |
| 83 | *two horse race* |
| 85 | *inevitability* |
| 87 | *shreds* |
| 89 | *spoons* |
| 92 | *spare room* |
| 93 | *thunderclap* |
| 94 | *Campo de' Fiori* |
| 96 | *mercy* |
| 97 | *each pale song* |

*previously uncollected*

| | |
|---|---|
| 101 | *nodes* |
| 102 | *gatefold sleeves* |
| 103 | *open day* |
| 104 | *bare feet* |
| 105 | *comes to rest* |
| 106 | *smoke stake* |
| 108 | *the telephone box* |
| 109 | *a sort of autumn* |
| 110 | *anything but cereal* |
| 111 | *bone patch* |
| 112 | *wheels are gods* |

*from* **pollen and the storm**

## **pedestrian**

in the possible hush
of 6am
the road is dusted
in pastel-smoke

feet bully the pavement
and cars slip down the highway.

on rubbish bins
crows flick glances
like struck matches

and the wind
squeezes by, rustling
plum blossoms
with clumsy arms.

## hazel

little girl sweeps herself
across the park
a pretty burn
of yellow cloth

highway steams
and the shovel handle
pricks the sky

once, twice, three times
he hacks the earth, rain
chasing arms
and the litter of autumn
shiny-brown.

## 31 Anderson Street

she took a long drink with her pill
unplugging the phone
and walking the footpath outside
up and down
the concrete warm
the gum dirty-smooth

she watched the cars
smoking
as she dragged in the evening,
pollen and the storm
coming unstuck, fluttering to the road
where she caught their scent.

she stood there with church-bells drifting over rooftops
sun diving, ink in her fingertips turning blue
and her arms wrapped in a cardigan
streetlights blooming, rain falling.

## odd

funny how odd socks
make me happy

but then, so does wind in my sleeves
or the printed word
and sun dried tomato

so do truly shabby
second hand bookstores
and a whole day without a phone call

so does chocolate that stings my teeth
rain on a tin roof
and your tattoo

funny how these things
are enough.

## sticks in milk

up in a plane
(the sea spilt below)
I'm hoping
that I don't end up
in some CSI knock-off
with hip music
and pigtails, with a goth
salivating over a pocket-watch gizmo
used for counting sperm

skin laid out
blue with frost
and teeth like signets

regrets seeping from my ruptures

and dreams
scattered
like scrap metal in the deep.

## storm

in the hall, Debussy
and grass seeds
blown in to slip
between floorboards

from the highway
an engine
melts into thunder,
clouds
with salt and pepper beards
hint at rain

and fence posts
lean, as though resting on rifles.

# churchill

sometimes the brittle air
at dawn
is swallowed by the shed,
grey planks with dew-stubble
and oil drums
slouching against
the side

almost hidden
by the bitter green of pine-trees
arms stretching for the road,
swiping log trucks
flinging needles to the wind

and sometimes, when
evening draws back the sun,
like a blanket leaving
skin, a cow groans
from the eye-socket window.

*from* **stepping over seasons**

## small town

has an old Esso sign on a tin shed
and someone who used to sell honey
painted yellow on the next one,

at the corner a pink golf ball
towers over the coastline, ridges
like the moon.

in spring flowers grow
round the blue tractor
and dirt collects in the seat

marks on the footpath
don't fade and the cemetery
never shrinks, only the town around it.

beyond the tennis courts
ghosts shed fingernails and
police sirens skip over fences;

no-one lives down there
where the surf plays dead
and moonlight walks on water.

## on the road

when you're driving
you don't think about what they'd find,
what they'd call
'personal effects'
if they found your body.

in a pad full of notes
from other crash sites

you'd maybe be:

black-rimmed glasses
hair just-cut
wedding ring
and silver watch,
a few empty water bottles on the floor
pegs, a collection of john forbes' poetry
purple suit-jacket
last year's crumpled registration sticker
and a golf club in the back,
the one you found in the front garden
one morning

and all you are now
is a question (is this guy a donor?)
or a sheet to be filled out
at the morgue

you don't ask yourself, when driving
what kind of jokes they'd make about you,

it might be just like TV,
maybe they'd think you should have had
your prescription checked

and which one tells your wife,
how do they decide? will they draw straws
plucked from a roadside littered
with windshield glass?
or maybe rock paper scissors,
maybe it's just a job
to them, same way your job
is just a job sometimes.

when you're driving
you don't think about
how, on the way there, they might
get back to whatever it was they were
on about before the call,
could be Carlton getting a thrashing
last night
whether Australia should boycott
Beijing, or a girl
the driver's just met, he likes her legs
and she's into acting

you don't think about
yourself just behind the glass
in the supposed repose of the white sheet,
belongings in a plastic bag:
one that's somehow meant to sum you up
or give comfort to loved ones,
as if whatever happened to be in your car
the day you died,
would be everything
to the people who'd just lost you.

## echidna

it was sunday and god was resting
while somewhere back home, you wept
over the steel in your arm

I took a walk along the cliffs
and watched the sea tear itself
into a million black squids.

## august rain

plucking courage
from somewhere
she's months into
this newest illness
still working still
somehow smiling,
everything passes
in grey sheets then
crumbles like yoyo
or a long landslide,
i'm awed, holding a
tub of vicks at the
bedside just giving
my brave face and
though it's wearing
out, there isn't any
thing else i have so
we make do with
that and settle into
sheets that smell so
much of eucalypt.

## all this ink

if I sit up tonight
and stifle my yawns with music
and if I write something
worthwhile, maybe I can take her
where the sky is cracked
ice, and it's beautiful
because we're together.
if I sit up tonight
arms cold, torso wrong
and typing about it,
rented, everything rented
maybe I'll come up with a way.
if I sit up tonight and all this ink
becomes poetry, I could point the wheel
to a place we've never been,
watch Venice sink a little more
or show you stability in three bedrooms,
and looking back, you wouldn't see
smoke stacks or the front door.

## other objects

my wedding ring is a plain silver
barrel band. same as dad's, very modest
and very hard to keep smooth,
with scratches I can't keep track of and
don't want to hide. it's no good pretending
the marriage is perfect, no use
hanging all our memories and every
step of the future on just one symbol. other
objects speak of love, too. the weeping
maple we've shifted to every house, the
cup we fill with knives and forks
or the handwritten address you gave me
the night we met, walking the city
and flinging orange peel into hedges, things
that endure, things that have lines
and marks to prove them.

## bianca

on the bus
two girls talk baby names.

*bianca*
is popular

and I wonder if
they know it's Italian for 'white'

and if they do
which 'white' do they have in mind?

is it the morphine
white of hospital walls
or the hard-working
plastic poly pipe
nestled beneath the sink?

could it be white like rabbits, robes
and weatherboard,

or milk and snow?
is it the white of a cloud
racing across sky

clever-marketing-ploy-white
of their iPods

or is it cherry blossoms nestled
against pink in spring?

## Bukowski and a wide range of landlords

some struggles are truly epic
like Bukowski
and a wide range of landlords

or the hopeless
but well-meaning sign, painted
officious red

*no alcohol in the CBD*

and beneath it a smashed
VB bottle
coloured like a rotting
SA uniform

and my brother
snickering as we walk by

*tastes like piss.*

## bitches brew

words drove him through ash tray hills
rolling by half-lame spirits
robed in holy blue

he was worried, the liar, his
golden arms
unwrapping
leather straps round the mule

hands anchors
cities
blood-red in bottles
of midnight, sipping the smog
and ladies' perfume

skyline
a panther's arc.

sometimes, he went up, swirling with the wish-
wash of
hallucination; stars
cracking into each other like marbles
hurled by swollen knuckles

once, at the gate,
bragging about loneliness
he made a bow out of blue ribbon
and hung it above her headstone
murmuring to the wind.

## eastern avenue

moon's hangover
hits the street in a splash of white,
outside the window
the transformer
is like a gargoyle, sitting
halfway up the electricity pole,
either too old
or too lazy to climb higher.

## farm

dawn comes like someone embarrassed
to bring bad news, sunlight
very soft on weatherboard.

in the horse's mouth even straw sleeps
and the earth holds perfume,
memory of rain on pine needles.

hills are bone-grey and a cold hand
massages the empty river, no prayers
swim this belly of dust,
no whispers to quicken fruit.

night looks down in a shower of moth wings,
headlights turn powerlines into silver webs
and cheeks go unshaven.

# botanic

1.
the park is full of photographers
and readers
ibis with black noses
and people who won't smile at me
and people who will

cicadas and crickets in hymn

a chinese couple
posing for wedding photos

by the river
and a fig tree that weeps
to the earth, medusa
in shackles of green.

2.
beyond the gardens
sirens tunnel through air

and streets hum with threats,
the casino is purple

and sandals
meet ash as leaves
tickle street signs

plum-soft
rain

and sunlight,
spread across buildings
dapple gentle
on brows
a monsoon of small change
trickling
in and out of vending machines
market stalls
and restaurants

while clear above them
construction
cranes make moves
while wind plays a mean
ballet with nests
while two 6s are stuck together
in a cafe
while deep in the river
lie bottles without caps
and bones of cod

then swiftly to shadows
in afternoon
where
bamboo stands together
full of gossip.

## by the curve

a teacup sits on the sink
shoe-brown
inside, imagined marks
where you held it,
not by the handle
but by the curve, to fit a palm
aching from winter

and the rest of the kitchen
looks a little strained –
ant-killers nest against
the foggy window and
cutlery stands like a palisade

but somehow your teacup
shrugs off pain
with a sweeping shadow
cast low over the dish-rag,
to me it looks like you might
return at any minute.

## the jacket

on the chair
there's a filthy spring jacket
light enough
to catch every stray hair

a landscape
deep with ridges
from weeks spent crushed
into couch cushions, an ant might
spend a season in exile
dragging a single
crumb like penance

how important tomorrow
becomes, for the moses
of this desert is
your jacket, its pockets
full of stubs and receipts

I could map out
days and weeks, movies
you've seen, coffee
at hudson's and gelati
for summer

in the jacket
you linger in traces
and I rake them with my hands,
collect every scent.

*from* **orion tips the saucepan**

summer night
a red seahorse
in the clouds

waiting for rain
cherry blossoms shrivel
on corrugated iron

leading me home
a jet's tail
in the blue sky

borrowing her scissors
barefoot
in the rosemary patch

shadows lengthen
spider webs
in every peg

docked
at the mud-puddle
sails of a butterfly

        half the night now,
        thinking about
        getting another biscuit

a half moon
has pulled the covers
up to its chin

midnight swim
slow blink of fishing rigs
out in the black

    easter monday
    fresh flowers
    on the roadside

      a splash of yellow
      stands against
      the firestorm

even this weed
has a little flower
for the sun

from wall to wall
graffiti
directs the traffic


legs all over
the chopping block
a spider


three cherry blossoms
in a polystyrene cup
the concrete still warm


orion tips
the saucepan
black falls out


the cleaner's blush
closing the top drawer


up from the desk
the moon tells me
time for bed

sneaking through the fence
last year's
blackberry patch


    autumn moon
    groan as feet
    hit cold tiles


        rock to rock
        the small bird
        looks so busy


    the fingernail moon
    never for some reason
    a toenail


nothing between
ghost-gums
but the wind

*from* **between giants**

## archaeological moment

a penny has come thousands of miles
to hibernate in the dirt

it's not worth much
but neither is it worth nothing

once we clean it in a glass of coke
and the royal head has a nose again

we take it inside, though the first one
to tire of it reaches for the Sega

later on I don't know which one of us
will take it to the front shed

where the Nissan lords it over dead flies
that gather in the window sill,

and hide the penny behind a landscape
mum and dad haven't unpacked

years later when moving house
and neither one goes back for it

the penny can close its tiny eyes
to wait for a more archaeological moment.

## **transitions**

the airport is a clone of another airport.
we are waved through.
our water is not.
a smile would tear the universe
into pebbles. it would hurt reputations.
I expect gasmasks.
travelators make you want to run.
we sit. often, we are sitting
and eavesdropping through no fault of our own.
voices travel – we should be envious.
it is not always that clean.
people sleep in whatever shapes their bodies
fall into. it is a horrid jigsaw of seats and flesh.
tank tops. head dress. jeans designed to fade.
the boarding pass is grave,
like communion bread.
announcements are goddess-like.
windows cover more square miles
than football fields.
food is.
hands get shopping-bag fatigue.
ball and chain luggage.
money changes in a shallow register.
euros become american dollars become dirham
become australian. water is regained.
transfer signs bloom at baggage claims.
everything is duty-free.

## birds still talking

even this late, with the sun peddling
downhill, birds are still talking
as warm bricks
leftover from noon
cook ants
and soothe the ache in my back,
watching the lid on the letterbox
swing, click and squeak

I am taking hope seriously
in weather this good, no jumper
and no shoes –
it's getting better for walks
along the river after work,
when all the mind can manage
is little sounds of appreciation,
when words would
only cloud things over, burden
everything with meaning.

## now in the night

now in the night
         peach
       with more sig
     nificance than a bible
 to a drunk
minister
mourning his dwindling flock
  in an age where
Jesus is digitally
encoded

& no pew
  can fit desk-chair-spines
    or hearts with wheels

now in the night
a chance at happiness
just to hear rain
  dancing on the roof
partying

magnificently, now in the night    a hand
  smooths hair
  spread across pillows
    gone to porcelain

  in wave after wave
  of moonlight

```
                              in
        &            now      the
                              night
cutting up a banana
to chase away sugar-filled
        dreams
        & finding signs
                in loose change
                        or
                    a patt
                    ern seen
                only when the sun
            hits the curtains just right

        we're both
        looking for the same thing –
we're just strung out on different predictions

                both right down there
                        on our knees
                        when we think
                no-one is looking.
```

## Keith Jarrett's scarecrow

his notes haunt the house
as I prepare to sleep, but it's ok. I like its echo
because I'm less alone
when listening in the black, having it broken
only
by strips of light
that slip in around the curtains,
that pour from streetlights
by the park, where the spider webs
wait for morning dew in rigid patterns
and cross walking paths
that I'll later cruise
in sandals that demand more pavement
and more summer.

I do not wake once he begins
and it might only be four minutes
before I'm dreaming
that single pillow in the middle of our bed
like a goodbye note,
wrapping my head softly
so all the disaster can bleed right out

and the whole time, the stereo stands across the hall,
turned down quite low
but with its little lights unblinking,
the perfect scarecrow for
bad dreams.

## man of cloth

somehow after you wear
my t-shirts
they seem softer,
smell better
and I don't want to take them back

being happy can be this simple
so I stand in the wardrobe
a little longer,
hold the cloth to my face.

## yellows

the city worries. its streets fill like ants before
rain. shopping bags shackle. the wind rustles
taxis. roads are liquorice chewed, spat into
lines. wheels hijack space, stray leaves take on
thuggish cigarette butts in gutters. ring-pulls
hitchhike. twenty-foot women skyscrape, sell,
sell, sell. lights remain tight-lipped. 'closed'
signs are never circles. glass cools. silver
sprinkles the hats, horn notes fight through the
ragged tap dance of trams. alleys leak. fast food
yellows everything.

## a table set for thousands #2

I have to let the words make mistakes,
dozens of them, years of them
tonnes of them
before
I can take them out to dinner,
introduce them to dangerous types
happy holidays, marriage ceremonies
gainful employment, theft of history
blood feuds
strange cousins
and salesmen with coins that sparkle
like wishes in fountains,
before
I send them to gods with shaven heads
or bookies lined up, pads in hand
and travellers with shirts open
blouses, glimpses of skin
and book-keepers
smirking in shadow
turning pages
sharing secrets with silverfish
and customers
eager to be invited
to a dance that leaves
ink stains in a tango
across the mind, eyes that blink back
an assault of meaning, jokes or
careless barbs
and claims that simply
cannot be true.

## man about town

who turns up to every party
late and slow
and seeks the bar
with an ant-eater for a face

who shakes but does not dance
who barely keeps sentences together
but instead leaves them
spread out between mouths
like washing hanging
on string between
old buildings in Europe

who makes up every cent
he's ever earned, who tears tissues
with earthy fingers
and fills the salad bowl with
the smell of rats

who is found hugging a pot plant
after the music stops,
who does not want to go home
and tried to eat every handshake

who wears American
highway-cop sunglasses and passes
out on the couch
between conversations, whose
pants come with black-hole pockets
for small change and fivers

who hits on girls in posters
and leaves lichen-like drool
on fluffy pillows

who is found the next morning
in the stairwell, stinking of the grave
and undergoing a terrible chrysalis
and twitching.

## stamped flat stamped

in my office between classes
I rage at flat things: the sea,
the land, the hard, flat dollar coin
and all its friends,
the road too short by far
and my feet, fingernails and thumbs
sleeping, none of them wings
I rage at the flat things
until my voice is stamped flat
stamped like the stamp of a soldier's liberating
boot; I rage until all my dreams are flat
I rage so quietly that animals come close
I rage so well that people congratulate me
I rage so far that distant mummies wake in
their glass cabinets, I rage at the rainbow slinky
just because it sits at my desk
I rage so that you notice and go away
I rage at flat things like the paper kipple
growing over me, I rage at words I cannot fix
I rage so deep that Hades lets Persephone go back
for more flowers and I rage so much that
it flattens my soul, now like a leaf
as it turns in the breeze,
and no-one left to chase it.

## windstorm

we switched the heater off
a couple of hours ago
and I'm listening to the wind
roar around the room, outside
it's pushing against the weatherboard,
dragging bad memories with it.
it feels like no-one could possibly
be happy out there.
not with all that awful
silence beneath the wind – it's all I can hear:
the glow of tvs in our street
smoke from chimneys, the neighbour
slamming a door and the cat snooping round gutters,
but no sounds. it's ridiculous, you're
only a room and a half away
but I feel alone, cut off from everything,
as if I could scream your name and
still the wind would erase me. I'm afraid
now, that you aren't telling me what you want,
that you're folding up your dreams, very neatly now
and slipping them into a card that could fit into any box
and I'm afraid I might pack them away in a rush
to get to my own, and that you'd love me
too much to make a sound.

## concrete buttons

the street was always a flat division
between my bed and the cemetery.
the mown grass of our front yard,
twenty-something meters from
weeds round the tombstones, never worried me
for some reason. perhaps it was the makeshift
cricket pitch with its green-bin wicket,
where it stood between me, the ghosts and
their leathery hands.
maybe it was the stunts, my little brother
standing on his bmx seat with arms spread wide,
or my own blue bike with back-pedal brakes
that left fish tails and dust everywhere,
at least until they sealed the road.
it probably never bothered me,
because my nightmares
were not of shivering skeletons
crossing a blade-white street at night,
but of things much more human.
from the elm tree
I would look down on concrete buttons of death,
and see with nothing but a child's eyes.

# ridges in the skin

it's doubtful that the sour woman
in the gelato shop
was in a mood
because of the thousands
of Capuchin monks
and poor Romans
buried across the street

she'd be used to looking
over to the doors

where five chambers
of pelvic bones,
vertebrae and shoulder blades
made into wings
and skulls stacked
in seven-foot cages
lay

where beside them in a small chapel
not even a knuckle bone

and where mass must wait
until we tourists
stumble back
to our warm hotels
with slack faces
and a lingering chill,
very much aware of the marrow
beneath our skin.

## one of the townsfolk

despite our closeness
after all the hours I've spent
at its feet
from childhood with sticky fingers
& wide pupils
to today, sneering at it from the couch
but still unable to switch it off
for good,
it waits
making no overtures
from plastic feet,
so still but still so predatory;
the remote, its sly little
Puck
its patience like an old, desert stone
waiting for rain.
it knows I will push, press
& stab at it with lazy fingers
circling
in an almost stoned
fish-bowl dance
& I wonder what the television gives me

not just the pleasant cut-outs
of the sitcom & their dependability
being so utterly unlikely
to change,
nor is it shameful joy
beamed in via predictable

celebrity-failures
or even the news
when all I seem to want is mild weather,
& so if I'm not David
then I'm one of the squashed townsfolk
& I know that whatever resistance
I put up
is hardly going to wrap up a Western
or save planet earth.

## **stubble**

in *A Fistful of Dollars* Clint Eastwood's stubble
is thick enough to hide deer
or slow-witted
prospectors

an entire town could crop up
in the hollow of a cheek
with a village square
and a well
in the nick from a razor

and in the unlikely event of a smile

panic as the forest
sways.

*from* **old stone: haiku, haibun & senryu**

church steps
lead to a beggar's cup
sunburnt tourists

   in the Botticelli room
   crowds around
   portable air conditioners

     shuffling over old stone
     the echo
     of tour guides

shadows on the courthouse
shouting
over the pram

silver screen groans
stretched across
another romantic comedy

     re-runs –
     the police chief
     is always balding

this year
instead of bushfire
big dragonflies


such orange –
nobody's flowers
on the roadside


old ice on the sill
how once
we could laugh


through the shutters
a single fly
carries the chug of boats


cameras jostle for position
Pompeii plaster cast


drying off
the bathtub sings
an awful song

you are trying to sleep
and I am Coltrane's sax
steeped in sound


night fishing –
two pelicans
just out of sync


reading a book
the ocean has been
on the same page forever


writing late
moths patter
against the glass

## en route

the ultra cheerful sound of *The Asteroids Galaxy Tour* chirps from the radio as our driver sets his tanned hands on the wheel. his sleeves are rolled up over the wrist, where a wealth of dark hair lives like localised forest. he does not move his shoulders much, but to roll them occasionally. twice he gestures to the green range of Monte Cerreto, to tell us that Amalfi is on the other side.

he does not mention the columns of smoke that pour from different spots on the mountain, coloured slow. they grow as if exhaled by dragons buried deep in the earth, perhaps smuggled over Byzantine trade routes from beyond the sea. we stare out the window, catch glimpses of bright scales glittering on waves

>   narrow way –
>   black garbage bags
>   tied to fences

## **temple**

Pompeii rains. its grey sky is mutated in cobblestones and wagon ruts glisten in the quiet. its stray dogs are patient, waiting for pizza. your runners look out of place. synthetic. flexible. I follow you to the brothel, where stone beds lurk in shadow. our guide jokingly describes the frescoes as 'menus.' the water has no memory. it is all in the earth. nothing is soft now

>    filling with jackets
>    and umbrellas
>    temple ruins

# Firenze

beneath the Duomo, cameras mill about like ants. their owners are most dutiful, clicking then looking. inside my skull are painted green and white stripes and when I look back, it is with some terror. I do not know if I wanted to go home. the air here is warm, eternal pink, as if trapped in a fairytale. the tourists are so alive, even as they kill the moment with SLR

>grand bells
>cross the rooftops
>our hands meet

## Vatican Blues

at each bottle-necked corridor it's one step forward, two steps back. the tour groups are a mass of wandering cattle, linked by their brightly coloured transistors. they bump into us, rigid, processional, lacking a sense of purpose and trampling ghosts of the past. occasionally an arm steals above the din and at its top, like a star on a Christmas tree, is the unblinking eye of a camera. it makes its theft and retracts in shame

>    sweat beads
>    we stake out
>    the open window

## night train

the train chews at the city with the click and clack of steel teeth, burrowing deeper to come face to face with man-made black. we do not shiver and we do not speak, unwilling to switch off long enough to look around. the stations pass like flick-book pages; yellow, orange, blue, white, red and bits of purple too. some of us cannot wait. we're already standing, feet ready to take us on a dance from platform to platform, moving moving moving making the shuffling music of panic

> so little room
> a woman's bra strap
> pressed against glass

## shade cloth

we ride our bikes everywhere and want sunburn for eventual tans that the girls will supposedly notice. no pale strips of winter-skin, no slip slop slap, no lectures from our doctors or parents. eventually more than the sun sinks in, and I begin duelling with thick globs of sunscreen. it will be the headline act next summer—that welcome grease, the hard-to-hold bottle, its smell mixing with the fabric in towels and the clean, clean sand

> diving from the rocks
> gold leaves spin
> on black water

## green skeletons

stems of new bracken are like the arms of green skeletons, bursting from the earth and up into a shock of hair. behind them, the older, brown ones have put up their complex, dry latticework. across a fallen trunk, moss roams like close-cropped afro. green scents mesh with freshly hewn dirt; my shovel uncovers grubs, almost nothing like their sugary counterparts. I've pulled back their blanket of earth and now they curl up tight, missing the dark

>    resting on my handle
>    even the fly
>    wants some shade

## **dovetails**

the workshop bears the unmistakable scent of sawdust, one my father still carries home in his flannelette shirts. it migrates between us, invisible wings sparkling where the sun has tripped through Perspex skylights. buzzing saws mimic an angry hive. machined timber is smooth, the burrs stack themselves in mutated reds and browns. they lurk like sullen teenagers with hair in their eyes and plans in their pockets. later my father will soothe them into feature-pieces or small coasters, treat them for heat and our obsession with coffee. they will grow flat and still, have no more frowns

>   not even a shadow on him
>   my sweat
>   follows the grain

*from* **VI**

# even frogs could be happy

she lifted a lady-of-the-lake
arm to rub
at smudges on sky
until it was clean again and the business
of rain was finished

and all the ponds were full
and frogs could be happy
and I was jealous of them

for just a short time
until she told me soothing things
and I slept on the couch
before sunset
and woke with stars tapping
their silver fingers
on the window

and then she was gone
and the house seemed to sag
with her absence.

## 3885

the clothesline
swings
in a dry wind

and the echo of our voices
runs
down from the river
to where I stand
in yellow grass
eyes fixed
on a horizon swollen with blue

the river
where we'd swim
through the black gold of the water
rapids
gnashing teeth
and water dragons
nimble
as we give chase

how sharp the bite
of the sun
who we would
more or less
worship for the entire season
no sand too hot
no bike seat too hard
no hole too far

and nothing
nothing
coming
even close
to lasting long enough

## pink oceans

here he goes
the boy
into the fairground
now
spitting, kicking spinning
bleeding
words
new words
little angry
fire-cracker words,
he's trying them on
with squeaks
and bright fists
those words
the ones
that belong to others
with bigger hands
workman-like
hands
hands of dark
grease and hair
and thumbnails
huge
moons setting
into their pink oceans
and all gone to hardness
now with the snarl of steel
and blooming fire

all forging
all holding
the usual panic
and promises
but mostly just holding
all the rage
he's trying to copy
down there
by the teacups
spinning their blue handles
into the night
as he paces
and plans
the crack of each word
hitting skin
and the hiss
of every syllable/
cutting deep.

## destined for mud

1.

there is a pulse
beneath this state of mind:

like a giant squid biding time
gills very patient
beneath water awfully black
and having melted softly

the car rolls to a halt.
through the trees no more than
a minute of light and then
headlights are clicked off

deep coffee sipped
from the dashboard
a spot of rain

as rats cross leaves
and an owl falls in white,
soundless as the samurai's blade
or the kiss for a sleeping
child's forehead.

the hammer jumps from the boot
and shoes go unpolished
that morning,
destined for mud in any case.

2.

now the engine
with its Tom Waits voice
heading back, flinging
dead animals
into collection-plate-ditches
beside the road

their funerals microscopic

and the speed-dial clock
glowing nuclear,
somewhere in the AM.

later, the raincoat is hosed down
behind a petrol station
with bright lights and sliding doors

in the glove box there is no such
hope.

3.

the wheels hardly blaze
and the handle
to wind the window down
bears a film of sweat

something interferes
with the dusty, country-death song
on the radio

and red sirens echo beneath clouds

that gobble constellations
like ugly worms

from the back seat
something stirs beneath a towel,
gurgles with love
or curiosity
and it makes no difference
to his rattlesnake eyes

## Beat Hero

the city's bones
have grown too thin
& your cigarette
thinks only of jazz

no-one matches
your wit
& somehow
you stake out new
territory
with each & every handshake

& later, many years later
after the clanging of trains
has stopped

you'll be sure you were happy

& if photographed you will
look just like a Beat hero

## super-8 sketches

how disappointing to remember so little.

my mind can sketch anything
in a saturated
super-8 flashback style but only for a few days
and months and years later the picture won't
have any detail at all,
no close-ups
or sense of movement,
and at best the soundtrack will be
like a pretty good cover band
and at worst
you won't even recognise the instruments

and no way, if you're looking to pause
something
don't bother, mate
since every frame just sort of floats off into ink
no matter which limb you press

and I miss the things
I used to think were mine

too many of my clips
are just gone
now, time chewing on them
like an earthworm working through pasture,
in through the eyes
and out the back of my head or something,
dissolving

dreaming dying
or already passing
in the chill of winter soil

and the deeper I dig
the thinner everything gets
until all the colour goes too
and my hands are buried in their manyfold
deaths.

## two horse race

whenever I
catch a glimpse of them warming up for
another round of backchat I
feel all the politics run out of me i
n cartoon speech bubbles filled with Z's and I

swear my tongue is now covered i
n revolutionary posters I
add moustaches and generous splashes of red
to them I
see the landscape of Coke and Pepsi
vying for position and I

am sick with the heavy, two-party apathy – thi
s bullshit is like a shovel-blow to the head and I
'm being offered a big fat price-reduction-
placebo ri
ght after and I

hate having no answers because I
like to fix things, even if I

admit, every one of my good intentions i
s more a fleet of oxen-like handymen but I
am determi
ned to set things right as I
trample things instead, well aware that I
move like a lost Stooges routine
and so after so many fai
lures I

stop

and end up making so little noise that I

well suspect my vote and my lines never stirred the water.

# inevitability

new frost ices the fields

and my footprints crunch
and my breath
ghosts

at the fence post
there's so much of empty beyond

even the grass
must be wondering
what happened
where did everyone go?

and there's no answer
beyond the inevitability
of decay

which has long crept up
on us
right down
to the laces of our boots
and the fraying of sincerity

and as I leave

the car becomes a bull
and chews on the road

black bits
getting
stuck between its teeth.

## shreds

if you're somewhere beyond
that keyhole
Alice-like maybe
or sleeping so soundly that
the thunder of
my chest collapsing
does not stir you
and if your pin-cushion veins
are the first things to
change
I want to see it
beyond the rustle of bed sheets
and quiet green bleeps
of equipment
so empty of love that they
must
have never been sad,
which isn't to say you haven't made me
happy – Christ no
it means only that their electricity
cannot grow lonely
and that it is never going to be a match for your
lungs

and if you don't wake
for many hours yet
I'll be listening from the kitchen,
my hands like dull spiders
on the cutlery and pots and dials

and I'll be listening
for the moment you stir
so I can smile as you wake
try to be strong
as you have been strong
for me
stronger than the pain
that
like a wretched ghost, wrings out
its song in the whisper
of your bones,
but a ghost you will nevertheless tear into a million shreds
and then release,
each one now thin enough
for the clouds to swallow.

## spoons

I want more for you –

more than medicine's
many-coloured pinwheel of side effects

like the shittiest fucking game show ever

give us something better than
nausea, migraines, depression
and
a dampening of symptoms
like the drip from an air-conditioner
pooling
in a rat-shit alley

give us more than appointments
to make other appointments
and the stab wounds of the bills
that go with them
as red blooms
in vase after vase of plastic flowers

until all I can see is red

because there's yet another test for you
to endure
simply
so the resistance of flesh to needle
might be measured again

or the effectiveness of radiation blocking gear,
that too

as we hit our maximum dose
for the 12-month period


I want more for you than I can give

and I know *it's no-one's fault*
a phrase that's like a prayer around here

but I know also, there's no medicine
no magic, no lottery for the things I want for you

classic things like:

routine
surety
looking ahead
the blessing of choice

little mongrels of things people
couldn't give a fuck about
until they're taken away and replaced
with glittering
consolations:

plan B
plan C
plan D
plan E

and on until we achieve true stasis just like
the bikini girl's smile

I want for you something better
than my powerlessness

I want to give you my spoons
as many as I can spare

I want to give you daylight without pain

a week where no gongs sing out new,
bizarre symptoms
phoned in from the executive producer
on the top floor

a day where you can simply run again!

criss-cross a park like a giddy butterfly

or maybe swing a racquet

maybe stand
maybe just be able to stand without
having to stand on daggers

or forget

forget

if I could give you a day at least, one day
where you didn't have to know
this is forever

## spare room

we'll call it the 'spare' room instead, I guess
there
where absence is found
and we'll both understand
that it's not empty truly


we take out the picture-books
and the little plastic toys
without specific names
– just toys really, some cheap, some cute
and all to be sealed in a larger
plastic coffin
and stuffed between other boxes
and tubs in the shed,
where we don't have to feel the same slice
each time our eyes slide across it

and what I think I'll leave behind
*must be more than bitterness*
or vicious, thin things that aren't quite prayers
or accusations
but instead, the hush of half-formed promises
I can later make to you face to face –
the idea that two is enough
and was never, not once, ever
                              not enough

# thunderclap

I do not have you
except in the half-dream
squeezed between a lunch break

and the next class
where you are asking me
to lift you up
onto my shoulders

who knows exactly
what colour your hair

or whether it would be winter
with frost lurking on bench seats

or whether I would
be gentle enough

and who knows
if I am writing this to naught
but a heroically white cloud
or whether you'd be
hiding in the coming spring

I cannot plan for your small steps

each a thunderclap
in my chest

## Campo de' Fiori

I chase you through the file extensions
littered across my computers
and with each little
*click*
you are enlarged
but I get no closer, salt in a wound
as the pixels
run
and I hit that X again
only to repeat the whole game
the next night,
in an aching chair
where moths are on loop
and the counterfeit moon
flickers
from inside the light shade,
it seems
now
that whenever I blink
you slip between the frames

and even in memory you fragment
as if the wind had been everywhere first:

gone

the taxi driver's face
but not his cigarettes
                gone

the rainbow of fruit but not the sun
where it punished Bruno's hood        and gone
the hundreds of cats
yet not the graffiti
worming
its way across yellow walls
                              gone
the tourists
but never the things we worshipped.

## **mercy**

linked by the bright blue of our lanyards
we form a kind statistically-varied
'blue team' tour group,
and into the Colosseum
separated only
by the distance of radio signal
and frequency of camera clicks
we go

climbing smooth stone
and moving through arches
passing brickwork
stripped down to its skeleton
by centuries of looters
whether Papal in nature
or committed earlier by dark-agers
desperate for brass

yet it's so easy to forget
smog-stains on the tiers
to look beyond
restoration scaffolding
where it clings like clumsy spider webs

and let my tour group fade,
let the great age of the place
overwhelm –
as so often in this city
I find myself completely
at the mercy of its echoes.

## each pale song

your hair has grown deep
into the green stone of age

just as hills have grown between us
and oceans salt everything –
sunbathers
and their pastel umbrellas
get away with nothing here

and driftwood piles
in hours
heaped upon
what few memories I have gathered

even as my head spills them
in a dance of clouds,
torsos thin,
each pale song
a gouge in my chest

but it is simple enough:
I want you

and now the statues have turned all
shoulders
tear-drop smooth

and the polish of feet
across your body,
how many is it now?

your hands were so wide,
as if to rival Atlas
who was always just out of sight
who was slowly unfreezing
and whose pulse
was seismic
but who could not fit you
within his stern gaze

and I will forgive every stumble
each scratch
each sour bite you give
when ignored
and even, envy so great
as to rattle my very bones

but you hid so well,
caught,
suspended
between a breath
and the settling of night

your sweet face

I wonder
did you ever truly need to paint it?

your own voice grew young
in my listening
and
I leant against cool railings
and you called me back to see
secrets
that were everyone's
but become ours

by the whispers I couldn't fully unearth,
as crowds of automated eyes
pillaged you
as I myself would later do
as so many could not resist to do
and what I kept
could never satisfy

your immortality dried
as we worked,
great deserts in our fingertips
and dust in our kisses

and though I cannot feel more shame
knowing that I want more

at least when change came
thank god
you were not part of its neon creeping.

# Uncollected

## nodes

bamboo grew in our backyard
somehow
or I imagined it
supple unforgiving
reliable, behind the shed
next to the pine
towering over rusted
tools and number plates

maybe I remember bamboo or something like it
at school
could have been in a book at home
that I borrowed from school

somewhere I tried to break it
with a child's hands
and insane, destructive curiosity
I wondered
how pandas could eat bamboo
(thinking sticks would hurt the throat)

it was probably a movie
or a reed at the river, where we leapt
from stone towers like
infant gods
testing, stupid, happy
in summer, futureless
and unconcerned

the bamboo must have been
wicker curled into a washing basket
on mum's back step.

## gatefold sleeves

the oarsmen shout
and the crash of waves
echo in their mouths

through so much black
the moon drops closer
for a better look

their buttons taste like salt

and the bunch of muscles
reminds me of my father
working with his saw

at home mum is cooking

playing Hawkwind while
I look at the LP, discovering
gatefold sleeves

the boat rolls around and
across parts of the water
their gifts are reflected.

## open day

the bus stopped by a river, banks
steeped in yellow grass
with a fence to keep
animals off the highway

but a fence that still let ants
slip through
and cover little corpses
like restless nets

the campus was still
an hour away
with its labyrinth
of faces and stone skies
shedding grey

we weren't to meet for four more years
and at a different university
but still
I thought about you, imagined
myself smart and happy
thinking the two went
together

and sat on the steps
of a great library,
feeling footsteps across my spine
like the spider of your touch.

## bare feet

through towns of peeling weatherboard
and lakes of fuzz
like a million detuned tvs,
I'm watching for dust on the horizon
thumb in my jeans as she
hums hallelujah, bare feet on the windscreen

up ahead
a husk of clouds
can't manage silver of the dirtiest spoon
not even the scuff
of feathers caught
in yellow grass beside the road

piano notes
chipping at the speakers
as rachmaninoff hits those heavy
Cs and we exhale
fog up the glass, cover up
secrets that wiggle like caterpillars.

## comes to rest

the dandelion clock roams
like a heart-beat fairy
over blackened trees
that reach from a seabed
   of green -
frozen shipwrecks
   spilling charcoal
from glorious wounds
and peppering the sand -
   each spore
thinner than mist,
comes to rest in
the smallest places.

## smoke stack

it was something between us       like a
smoke stack
or a hundred miles of fat pasture
eggs cooking in the den      and cows vicious
in the yard

young hands mixing concrete, spiders in furry
vests and funny little names for her friends
                tap dancing
horse racing

the house crowded      floorboards racking up
records and paint
- a loose green curtain      separating
the music and the children
from the adults      smoking      serious
and happy
unaware that in ten years – divorce

there was no light
beneath millions of fingerprints on the
windscreen

and it wasn't the orange sun or the glass with
the crack in the handle
it was something between us      like a
snow storm     flakes
dragging themselves up to your feet.

## the telephone box

high on mount livingston
a telephone box
sits beside the broadcast tower
and does nothing
or does what a set-piece does,
once you're really close
you see that total lack of functionality

but it looks good.
kind of dr.who-ish, with serious
panel windows and a roof-facade
that could have been carved marble
but is in fact
concrete.
best of all is fetching black and yellow
lettering that says TELEPHONE
in a manner that demands you
step inside
and immediately
shed
clark kent
or at least dial for don adams.

## a sort of autumn

I spend so much time
worrying about the impermanence
of things I love, that they slip
into a sort of autumn
in my mind, I'm wasting time
by missing something I can still touch

so I have to slip into bed tonight
without waking you
and stroke your back, let you know
I'm there, without spoiling the moment

in a darkness made incomplete
by red numbers of the alarm clock,
I have to remind myself
not to count everything.

# anything but cereal

part of me is waking up at ten to seven
and opening the gate
forcing myself to eat breakfast –
anything but cereal

and on the back step
where the laundry exhales
part of me plays a little guitar
till the fret wears down the 'e' string
and cuts my finger

part of me is throwing cds onto the backseat
and filling the car with petrol,
my atm card juvenile-blue,
wedding photo in wallet

and lunch something with cheese
as rain hits glass
with thousands of fingers,
very, very close to impolite

part of me is repeating these things
until I'm worn in
deep grooves
like a walking path over new grass,
until all that's left are flecks of
dreams like paint scraped
from walls.

## bone patch

this house is made for
our bones, with grooves where
the right things rest

such as ankles in couch cushions
or invisible targets
for my elbows, when I
lean on the kitchen bench
to watch your magic

or the dip in our bed,
where bossy hip bones have
carved out so many dreams
from the old fairy floss
of our mattress

right down to the small bits
like the hair tie
gone missing in the laundry,
a thin python for your wrist.

## wheels are gods

so onto the highway
looking forward now
daylight blessing the dashboard
and road-signs falling down
cicadas drunk, singing
the same lines over
and over – rainbows trapped
in webs between garbage cans
in suburban streets
after long nights of
being still and the haggard faces
of clouds drooping over rooves
rain like the echo of
a thousand fists on locked doors
and we're just about across
the state line
and the keys are light
and petrol stations rise up on
an orange horizon, tall as
saints settling on earth.

# Also by Ashley

*pollen and the storm*
*stepping over seasons*
*orion tips the saucepan*
*between giants*
*old stone: haiku, haibun & senryu*
*7 Years*
*VI*

www.ingramcontent.com/pod-product-compliance
Lightning Source LLC
Chambersburg PA
CBHW020902020526
44112CB00052B/1192